THE STORY OF
PASSOVER

by David A. Adler

illustrated by Jill Weber

HOLIDAY HOUSE / NEW YORK

For Renée, the ultimate holiday hostess—D. A. A.

For Renee, because my favorite Passovers were spent at her house—J. W.

The publisher would like to thank
Rabbi Frank A. Tamburello for his
expert reading of the text and art.

Library of Congress Cataloging-in-Publication Data
Adler, David A.
The story of Passover / by David A. Adler ; illustrated by Jill Weber. — 1st edition.
pages cm
ISBN 978-0-8234-2902-8 (hardcover)
1. Passover—Juvenile literature. I. Weber, Jill, illustrator. II. Title.
BM695.P3A3425 2014
296.4'37—dc23
2012045839

ISBN 978-0-8234-3304-9 (paperback)

The story of Passover begins more than three thousand years ago when Jacob and his family settled in Egypt. Jacob was called Israel, and his family were called the Children of Israel. They were also called Hebrews because of the language they spoke.

Many years passed. Jacob
and his children had all died.
To the pharaoh, the ruler of
Egypt, the Children of Israel were
outsiders. He was afraid that one
day they would rebel. To
control them, he made them
slaves. He forced them to
do hard work. They were
beaten. Some were killed.

The wise men of Egypt told the pharaoh that one day a Hebrew boy would be born who would lead his people against Egypt. They couldn't tell him which boy it would be, so the pharaoh decreed that every newborn Hebrew boy must be thrown into the river and drowned.

One boy was saved.

At first his mother hid him. Then when he grew too big to hide, she placed him in a small basket. She put the basket in the river. The baby's sister Miriam hid nearby to see what would happen.

A princess, the pharaoh's daughter, found the baby. She named him Moses and planned to raise him as her own child.

Miriam ran to her.
"Should I get you someone
to help you with the baby?"
"Yes," the princess said.
Miriam brought the baby's
mother to work in the palace.
Moses was adopted by the
princess, but he knew he was
one of the Children of Israel.

When he was a young man, he saw an Egyptian beat a slave. Moses attacked the Egyptian and killed him. Then he ran away.

Moses settled far from Egypt.
He married and worked as a shepherd.

One day, while Moses was watching his
sheep, he saw a burning bush. There were
flames, but the bush wasn't harmed.

"Moses, Moses," a voice called from the bush.

"Yes, here I am."

God spoke to Moses from the burning bush.
He told Moses to lead the Children of Israel
out of Egypt.

Moses and his older brother, Aaron, went to the pharaoh. They asked him to let the Children of Israel go free.

The pharaoh refused. He forced the Children of Israel to work even harder.

Moses and Aaron warned him that if he didn't let the Hebrews go, the waters of Egypt would turn to blood.

The pharaoh refused, and the waters turned to blood.

That was the first plague
to strike Egypt.
There were ten.

Frogs covered the land.

A thick cloud of lice
swarmed over Egypt.

Animals ran wild. The Egyptians' cattle became terribly sick and died.

Painful boils broke out on the
skin of the Egyptians.

Huge hailstones mixed with fire
fell on the land.

A swarm of locusts attacked Egypt.

It was as dark as night in the middle of the day.

Then came the tenth plague.
One by one, the firstborn Egyptian
sons died. The Angel of Death only
visited the homes of the Egyptians.
He passed over the homes of
the Children of Israel.

The pharaoh was frightened. He was a firstborn son. He called for Moses and Aaron. "Leave now," he told them. "Go quickly before we all die."

The Children of Israel left that very night.
The next day the pharaoh had a change of heart.
He and his army chased after the former slaves.

The pharaoh's soldiers had horses, and their chariots were getting closer and closer to the Children of Israel. The Red Sea was in front of them. The soldiers were behind them. They seemed trapped.

God told Moses to lift his stick and to spread his hands over the sea. Moses did, and the sea divided. The Children of Israel walked through the sea on dry land.

The pharaoh's army followed them. Then when the soldiers were in the midst of the sea, Moses raised his stick again. The waters flooded together. The Egyptians drowned, and the Children of Israel were free.

On Passover, Jewish people all over the world celebrate their freedom from slavery and their beginnings as a great nation.

THE SEDER

The name of the holiday, Passover, was taken from the tenth plague, the deaths of the firstborns. The Angel of Death only visited the homes of the Egyptians. He "passed over" the homes of the Children of Israel.

Passover lasts for eight days. On the first night of Passover, and in traditional Jewish homes outside Israel on the second night, too, there is a special seder meal. It begins with an invitation and a prayer. The invitation is for anyone who is hungry to come and join the seder. The prayer is that in the coming year, all slaves will be set free.

Children are encouraged to ask questions at the seder and to listen to the story of Passover.

At the head of the table is a seder plate. On it are symbols of the day.

There's a vegetable and salt water for dipping. The salt water is a reminder of the tears the slaves shed.

The *moror*, bitter herbs, on the plate are a small taste of the bitterness of slavery.

Charoset is a clay-like mixture of apples, nut, spices, and wine, a reminder of the clay the slaves molded into bricks.

The roasted bone is a reminder of the Passover sacrifice.

There's a roasted egg on the plate. An egg represents the Children of Israel. It's the only food that gets harder, not softer, the longer it's cooked. And in Egypt and throughout the generations, the greater the oppression, the more the Children of Israel held on to their beliefs.

On the table, too, is matzoh, a flat kind of bread. The Children of Israel left Egypt so quickly, the bread they were baking did not have a chance to rise. Matzoh is the kind of bread they ate.

Everyone at the seder gets to drink four cups of wine or grape juice. When the talk of the ten plagues begins, some wine is spilled in memory of the Egyptians who died so the Children of Israel could be free.